One Mezuzah

A Jewish Counting Book

CAROL KITMAN
ANN HURWITZ

ROSEL BOOKS

preschool

ACKNOWLEDGMENTS

Thank you to Floreva Cohen, Ruth Musnikow, Rivka Behar, and Vivian Horowitz of the Board of Jewish Education and to Jack Snyder for pointing us in the right direction. Special thanks to Charles Lieber and Bill Krasilovsky for their good counsel. We are grateful to Rabbi Zelig Block for the loan of his shofar and spice box and for permitting us to take photographs at Temple Sons of Israel, Leonia, New Jersey. We are also grateful to Judith Tumin, Educational Director of the Society for the Advancement of Judaism for lending us their teaching Torah. We were fortunate to have the assistance of Elaine Schule, Rosa Jaffe, Leonid Vindman, Jessie Glass, Margaret Haynie, Lee and Diana Soorikian, James Weisberg, Marvin Kitman, Marshall Hurwitz, and Harriet and Tal Colen. Our thanks to the teachers of Bronx House Nursery School for their patience and support; also to Natalie Robins, Virginia Buckley and Robin Brancato for their time and guidance. We are grateful to Beatrice Aubrey, Ada Rivera, Kerim Friedman, Susan Sawyer, Claire Arbeiter, Nancy Ignall, Nicole Elliott, Wendy Rosoff, Elizabeth Pinto, Sandi Chace, Patricia Tighe, Ingrid Holm-Olsen and Megan and Colleen Hillery for their participation.

We could not have done the book without the three wonderful families who always gave more than we asked in a spirit of warm-hearted generosity and cooperation: the Glass family —Charles, Janet, Jessie, and especially Lara; the Lerman family — Bob, Emily, Heidi, and especially Jennifer; the Vindman family — Semyon, Ludmilla, Leonid, Alex, and especially the twins Alexander and Eugene who traveled so far to be with us.

Book and cover design by Vincent Tartaro

Manufactured in the United States of America

One Mezuzah

A Jewish Counting Book

DEDICATIONS

For my parents, Kate Perloff and Alter Sibushnick.
Carol Kitman

To my husband, Marshall, and my son, James.
Ann Hurwitz

One   אַחַת

1

One mezuzah
on the doorpost
to remember
One!

Two candles

Two שְׁתַּיִם

2

Two candles
lit at dusk
to say
"Shabbat Shalom."

שַׁבָּת שָׁלוֹם

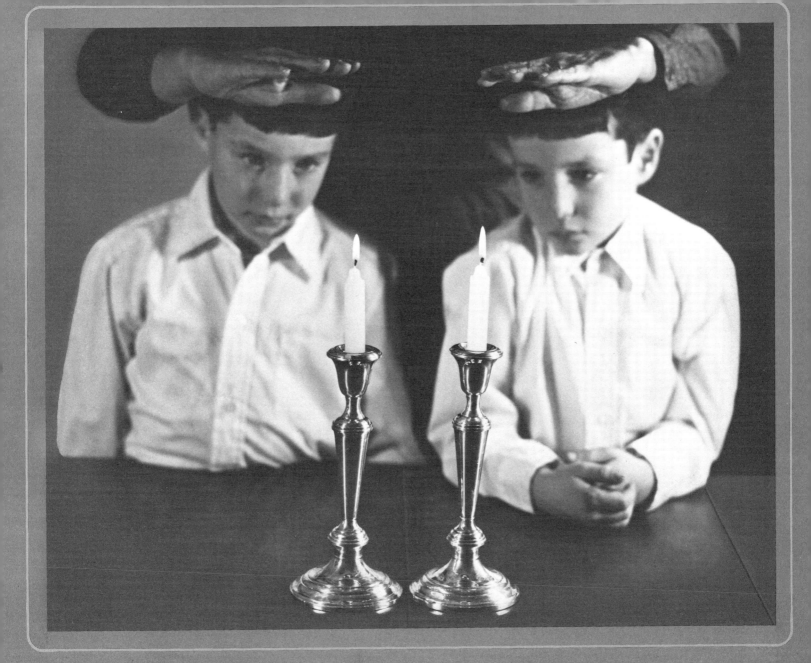

Three hamantaschen

Three   שָׁלֹשׁ

3

Three hamantaschen
on the plate
to taste
a happy Purim

פּוּרִים

Four questions

Four   אַרְבַּע

4

Four questions,
and four ways to ask,
"Why is this night different?"

פֶּסַח

Five Books of Moses

Five חָמֵשׁ

5

Five Books of Moses,
Tree of Life,
the Torah is our story.

תּוֹרָה

Six   שֵׁשׁ

6

Six days to make the world.

Six days to work,

to bake and weave and build and draw,

to light a fire and tie a knot.

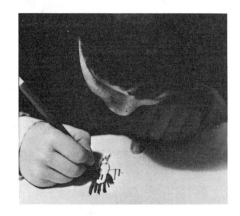

Seven synagogues,
houses of prayer and learning.

Seven   שֶׁבַע

7

Seven is a blessing —
Shabbat—the seventh day.
A time to rest and read
to sing and laugh
and pray.

שַׁבָּת

Eight   שְׁמוֹנָה
8

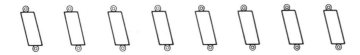

Eight nights of Hanukkah,
The Feast of Lights,
to warm
the winter dark.

חֲנֻכָּה

Nine pieces of apple

Nine   תֵּשַׁע

9

Nine pieces of apple

dipped in honey —

to taste for a sweet New Year.

רֹאשׁ הַשָׁנָה

Rosh ha-Shanah!
Let the shofar sound
for the birthday of the world.

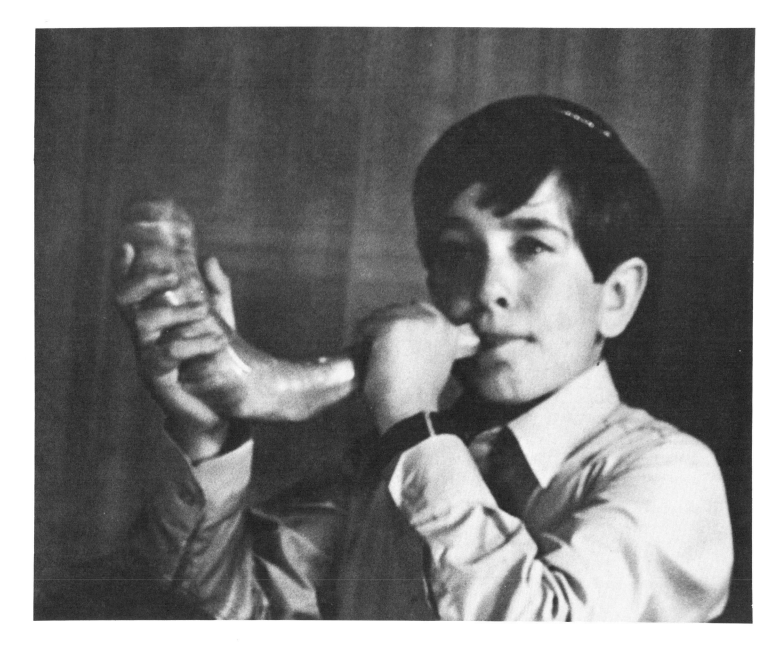

Ten   עֶשֶׂר

10

Ten fingers stand
for Ten Commandments,
rules to learn and keep.

עֲשֶׂרֶת הַדִּבְּרוֹת

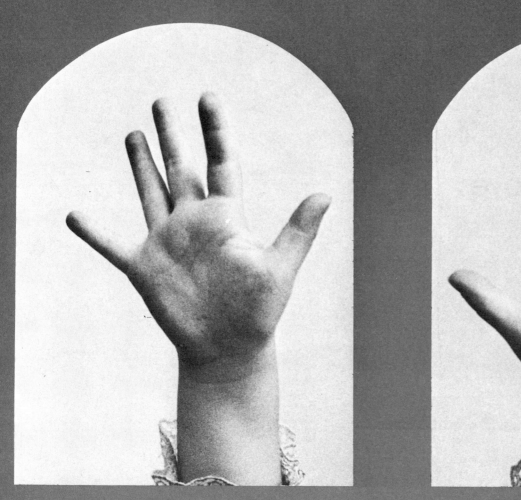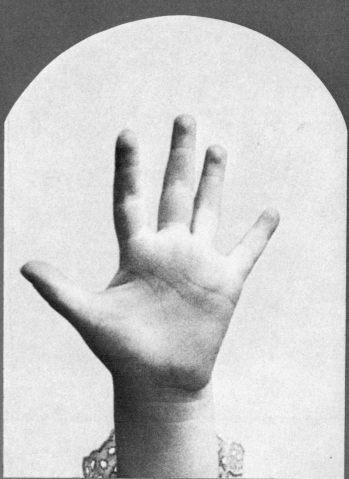

Eleven cloves

Eleven   אַחַת עֶשְׂרֵה
11

Eleven cloves for the spice box —
"Shalom, Shabbat, farewell."
The stars begin to light the sky,
it's time to make Havdalah.

הַבְדָּלָה

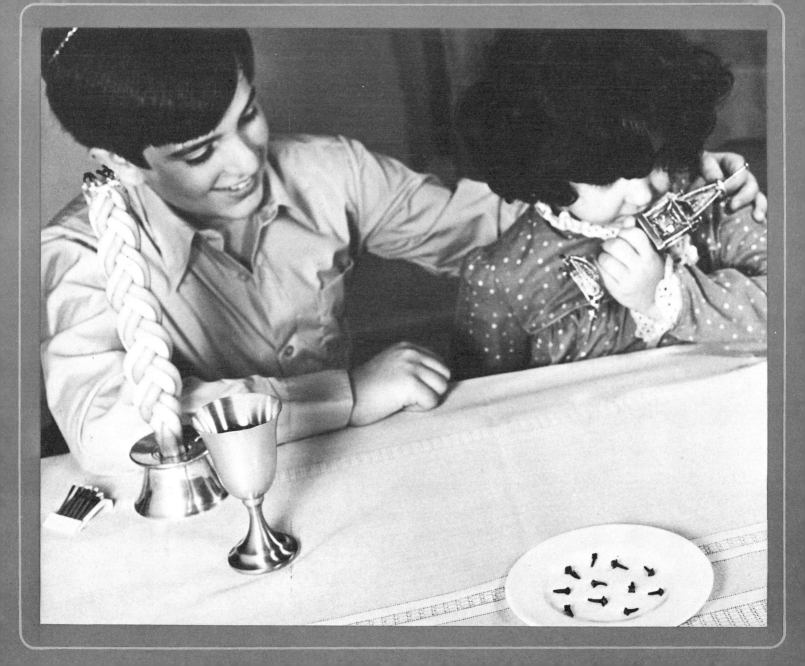

Twelve   שְׁתֵּים עֶשְׂרֵה

12

Twelve girls together,
sisters, cousins, friends,
rejoice and dance the horah.

הוֹרָה

Thirteen שְׁלֹשׁ עֶשְׂרֵה
13

Thirteen years old,
strong in heart and deed,
he stands to read from Torah.

בַּר מִצְוָה   בַּת מִצְוָה

Going out and coming in,
thirteen is a new beginning
for years of Jewish living.

Photo by Suzy Kitman

Carol Kitman grew up in the Boro Park section of Brooklyn. She attended the Sholem Aleichem Folkschule until she was 15. Her first camera was a high school graduation present. She earned a B.A. in History and Education from Brooklyn College and an M.S.E. in School Psychology from CCNY. She decided to become a full-time photojournalist after working for several years doing psychological testing and evaluation. She lives in Leonia, New Jersey, with her husband, Marvin; and has three grown children, Jamie, Suzy, and Andrea. This is her first book for children.

Ann Hurwitz was born in New York City. She attended Antioch College and received a master's degree in Early Childhood Education from Teachers College, Columbia University. She is currently the Director of Bronx House Jewish Community Center Nursery School and Kindergarten. Although this is her first published book, she has written stories on Jewish themes for the children with whom she has worked. She lives in Leonia, New Jersey, with her husband, Marshall; and has a grown son, James.

The authors who live across the street from each other had a good time working on this book together and with all of the children in the photographs.